DATE DUE

GOING HOME AWAY INDIAN
by
Leo Romero

Ahsahta Press
Boise State University
Boise, Idaho

Some of these poems first appeared in **Crosswinds**, **Fish Drum** (special cassette edition, 1990), **Northwest Review**, and **South Dakota Review**.

Editor for Ahsahta Press: Dale K. Boyer

Going Home Away Indian is printed
on acid-free text and cover pages.

ISBN 0-916272-41-9

Library of Congress Catalog Card Number:
89-80859

Contents

Introduction

Leo Romero's poems are stamped by the Southwest. But they're character-ized as much by a wild originality. They can be romantic, funny, and mysterious at the same time. And they sound like no one else's poems. Romero's land-scapes and characters are clearly Southwestern. He uses allegorical narratives and supernatural characters and incidents naturally, as one who grew up with *cuentos*, legends, and myths might be expected to do. But he transforms these traditional, regional elements. His romantic, zany imagination working through a language that is simple and understated—almost flat in places—concocts a poetry that makes one laugh and wonder, often simultaneously.

This unique style Romero has been developing over the years, but his peculiar mixture of romantic, comic, and surreal didn't reach full fruition until **Celso,** his collection of poems that focuses on the character Celso, wise fool and lecher, poet and wino of a northern New Mexico village. Through Celso, Romero voices typical New Mexican Hispanic folk-beliefs while satirizing the foibles of the villagers and meditating on love and death—all in a style that is simultaneously lyrical and comical, surreal, commonplace, and rapturous.

The poems in **Going Home Away Indian** continue in the style of **Celso.** The focus is now Native American culture rather than Hispanic. There is more political bite in some of these poems, an underlying—sometimes explicit—criticism of America's treatment of the Indian. But the writing style and mixed tone are characteristic. Here in place of the character Celso are the more sur-realistic characters Skeleton Indian and Marilyn Monroe Indian, a Navajo and a Pueblo who are lovers even though they are dead. Their death is, strangely, vital, an affirmation of their authenticity, their refusal to compromise to white American culture. At first described from a distance by an omniscient narrator, these characters begin to take on fuller life and speak for themselves. By the end of the book the poems are no longer narrated but have become fully dramatized conversations among the two Indian characters and the narrator, a Chicano, who has by this point been turned into a third character.

This is the character Raymond, who suddenly appears on the scene in the final section of the book. Raymond, a poet, is presumably the narrator of the first two sections. He can now appear on an equal footing with the two other dead characters and interact with them because he has just died himself. The poems in this section begin to function like brief chapters in a love story, slow-ly unfolding the love triangle in which Raymond competes with Skeleton In-dian for Marilyn Monroe Indian's love. These poems are less critical and satirical than the poems in the first two sections; instead they speak personally and philosophically on themes of love and death.

Romero also seems to be contemplating the act of writing itself in this final section—perhaps as he realizes regretfully that his book is coming to an end.

In some of these last poems one feels that Raymond is actually a manifestation of Romero himself, who, having created these characters, now wants to join them and remain with them. This impossible, beautiful desire is characteristic of Romero's romantic, surrealistic imagination, an imagination that sparks this book throughout and transforms familiar Southwestern elements into fascinating creations.

Joseph Somoza
Las Cruces, New Mexico
December 1989

For Elizabeth

I

He's Not As Friendly

He's not as friendly
as you would expect
an Indian to be
Or would you expect
an Indian to be
friendly
Anyway, he's got red
all around him
like a thin crust
Red like a red flannel shirt
from 1846
You can't see it
you say
It's there, I tell you
And you see the blue
beneath it
That's the real him
Not the blue
like the nearby sky
but the blue of far away
You can't see that either
you say
Look here
This Indian
is mighty angry
with you
He just looks friendly
Kinda
But I can see it
all coming out of him
Out of the deep blue
of him
Into the red

Going Home Away

Going home away
Indian
is what he calls himself
And I got no horse
to ride, he says
And If I did
I wouldn't ride it
I would walk alongside it
as if it were my buddy
Funny faced buddy
with big horse teeth
and big horse ass
I walk on home always
he says
and away
Secure in my green
cocoon blanket
And even if it were raining
fire
I'd walk on home
and away

He Was Dancing the Yellow Dance

He was dancing the Yellow Dance
with six others
All of them wearing
some yellow
Not too many people
like to wear yellow anymore, he thought
as he danced
This is a way of going
he thought
The yellow path of dancing
The sun's footsteps, he thought
We're dancing for
and with him, he thought
They danced all night
but to them it was like day
Dancing the Yellow Way

Again I Find Him

Again I find him
at the bar
drinking a beer
When did I leave you last
I ask him
Last was yesterday
he says
not offering to
buy me a beer
Was it only yesterday
I say
He doesn't say anything
Just into drinking
today
I can see the purple
talk is out of you
I say
He still doesn't say anything
Just looks straight
ahead
with sunglasses on
in this dark bar
The purple talk, I say
that's what you were
talking up
the last time I saw you
He doesn't say anything
to that
Oh, hell, I'll buy
myself a beer
I say out loud
You cheap sona bitch
Mesican, he says
out of the corner
of his mouth
You acting like a Navajo
now, I say to him
Hell, we Pueblos
could kill Mesicans too

he says
Like hell you could
I say
We grow quiet
and brood
Our beers
just a fist away
All the purple talk
talked out of me

He Didn't Like Me

He didn't like me
the first time
he saw me
He didn't see me
a second time
but I knew
He wouldn't have liked me
a second time
He was a Marine Indian
with all his hair
cut off
Why you hanging out
with this Mexican
I could see him thinking
as he talked with his brother
He seemed sore at his brother
Maybe it was because his
brother wore long braids
like an old time Indian
He was a new time Indian
Sore as hell at everyone
Except his uniform
and the Marines
That saved him
from he's not sure what
Oh, yeah
Saved him from hanging out
with Mexicans
and wearing his hair long
like a traditional
Indian

It Was In 1856

It was in 1856
he had his head
blown off
Direct hit
by a man
shooting
out of the train
at the buffalo
That was his worst
nightmare
He was dressed
in war regalia
A one man war party
And before
he could put an arrow
in his bow
The man turned
from aiming
at a buffalo
and aimed
at him

If Marilyn Monroe

If Marilyn Monroe
had been an Indian
would she have still
been considered
sexy
And would she
have become
a movie star
perhaps playing
the part
of a squaw
being raped
and massacred
over and over
in movie after movie
with many close-ups
of bare breasts
and thighs
Would her hair
still have been
as golden
And would every man
in America
have wanted
to make love
to her
when their wives
weren't looking
Would she still
have made teenage
boys
grow old with longing
even if she spoke
in a tongue
no white man
could understand
and had ancestral
memories
of being driven
into a tiny corner

of America
Would America
have forgiven itself
for what it did
to this Indian
Marilyn Monroe

In His Dreams

In his dreams
he rode naked
on a purple horse
Without a saddle
He held tight
to the mane
Naked wild Indian
in his dreams
with long braids
flailing
the prairie wind
But it's not
the prairie
he races across
but the ocean
A wide, endless
ocean
Leading his steed
westward
like the sun
A steed too wild
to tame
except in dreams
Racing
to awake
the nations
out of their
deathly slumber
A dream awakening
a sleep
out of its
nightmare

Skeleton Indian

Skeleton Indian
He wears blue jeans
he wears a red
oxblood
colored shirt
He wears sunglasses
even when it's night-time
The women do come out
in the night-time
They see him coming
Hey, Indian man
they say
We think you're cute
Skeleton Indian
grins at this
Cute, he says
Marilyn Monroe
is cute
Don't be offended
the women giggle
We see you're
manly
Big brave as you are
Still, cute is fine
for a man to be
And who's this
Marilyn
you're always
jabbering about
If we ever see her
we'll tear her dress off
and then some
Skeleton Indian
laughs out loud
Marilyn Monroe
is my skeleton woman
She's not afraid
of any alive
plump women

like you
Many a woman
has tried
to scratch out
her eyes
but she hasn't got any
Skeleton Indian
won't mess around
with these barfly
women
when he's got
Marilyn Monroe Indian
at home

Marilyn Monroe Indian

Marilyn Monroe Indian
Luscious cactus
fruit lips
Tight sweater
and tight
black pants
She's got a movie star
look about her
Wind blows up
her dress
and everybody looks
Especially the women
What's she got
that we ain't got
they whisper among
each other
White man approves
of such shapely legs
You're going out
on the town
to Manhattan's
and Los Angeles's
fanciest
You couldn't do
any better
than with
Marilyn Monroe Indian
by your side
Beautiful as she is
she can even read
palms
And no one doubts
her acting abilities
anymore
Me, she says modestly
How could all this
fame
come to me

Little girl
who grew up barefoot
on the reservation
By way of explaining her
other Indians say
she belongs
to the long lost
tribe
of albino Indians
out by Zuni
or someplace

Having His Head Blown

Having his head blown
off
is a recurring dream
he's had
since the first days
he went off to
Santa Fe
Indian School
He would look out
the window
at busy Cerrillos Road traffic
and long for
the Hopi mesas
How he would help
his grandfather
look after the corn
and keep an eye
for invading
Navajos
And the tourists
who came to buy
pottery
all looked funny
Now he was in a city
full of those people
and they were
scary
The first night
away
he had the dream
It was the early days
Even before
his grandfather
was a little boy
Navajos, he was
about to yell
from his rock perch
But just as he
opened his mouth

his face shattered
Lucky hit
he thought
When he woke up
he wrote a letter home
I hope you beat off
them Navajos
he wrote
And as a P.S.
he added
If a Navajo
reads this letter
You should be
ashamed of yourselves

Skeleton Indian He's the Talk

Skeleton Indian
he's the talk
of the town
from hogan
to Pueblo
to tepee
to apartment complex
in Albuquerque's
SE heights
Skeleton Indian
he's the talk
of the town
in his
turquoise colored
boots
and Arrow shirts
This is no
government Indian
He's an escaped
Indian
No reservation
can hold him
for long
Indian girls
tell Skeleton Indian
Take us away
from the wide open
spaces
of reservation life
Girls in Indian schools
say
Take us away
from grades
and future days
as office workers
and computer operators
Take us away
they all ask him

Even urban Indians
make eyes at him
Take us to where
we haven't been
they're always
asking him
Skeleton Indian
just smiles
As much as a skeleton
can smile
that is
He doesn't mind
all of the attention
Being the talk
of the town
and all

I Ever See You

I ever see you
in this bar again
he says
and I'll turn you
into a high
squeaky Mexican
A Mickey Mouse
of a Mexican
you hear
he says
This is an Indian bar
No Mexicans allowed
And if I ever see you
with an Indian woman
again
he says
I'll introduce
you to my friend
Skeleton Indian
before I kick
your butt
into the grave
Scary Indian he is
He scares Indians
half to death
without meaning to
Mexicans
he don't like
His dad was killed
by a Mexican
He comes around
after 11 o'clock
Any Mexicans
around here
he'll say
What's your name again
Martinez or Romero

What's that
Rodriguez
I'll remember
I won't forget
to introduce you
to Skeleton Indian
He won't like you
I can see
it's going
to be
a fun night after all

Yellow Blouse Woman

Yellow Blouse Woman
I called her
She didn't appreciate that
Didn't even really have
an Indian name
until she named herself
Part Indian, part white
She had come to see herself
more and more
as an Indian
I didn't mean any harm
calling her Yellow Blouse Woman
It was almost the only blouse
I'd see her wear
Not quite
There must of been others
She wasn't that poor
And there was always Goodwill
and Salvation Army
But I swear that's all
I'd remember
And I see it still

Skeleton Indian He Smokes

Skeleton Indian
he smokes
a cigarette
He smokes Kools
He smokes Camels
He doesn't much care
what he smokes
And he puffs like mad
Hey, people yell
Your face is
on fire
Smoke signals
that's what
Skeleton Indian
is doing
He's sending
smoke signals
but people don't
understand them
anymore
But he keeps
sending them
There's no other way
to say
what he has
to say
For all his outward
appearances
His sophistication
Skeleton Indian
is really
a back hills
Indian
Take off his fancy clothes
and what do you have

Skeleton Indian Thinks

Skeleton Indian
thinks
if anyone offered
to paint his portrait
it'd become
as famous
as the Mona Lisa
No lips
how does he smile
with no lips
people would ask
The painting
would sell for the millions
and some eccentric
Japanese would keep it
hidden
in Tokyo
And Skeleton Indian
would chuckle about it
You know what
that Jap does
Skeleton Indian
would say
He shows the painting
to the most privileged
class in Japan
and whispers to them
That's a painting
of a code talker
That's why we lost
the war
They had death
on their side
Skeleton Indian
would die laughing
from this
if he wasn't
already dead

Mona Lisa Indian
That's him
Leonardo
who's that
A code talker
Skeleton Indian
chuckles

Skeleton Indian Was a Navajo

Skeleton Indian
was a Navajo
when he was alive
Still am
says Skeleton Indian
No difference between
a live and dead Navajo
Still Navajos
And Marilyn Monroe Indian
was Pueblo
when she was alive
Still am
says Marilyn Monroe Indian
No difference between
a live and dead Pueblo
Still Pueblos
A great nation
of the living and the dead
she adds
Just like the Navajos
How is it you two
get along so well
Him being Navajo and all
I ask
Skeleton Indian
gets angry at that
Why is everybody always
picking on the Navajos
he says
We've suffered enough
for our raiding days
Driven away from our home
by Kit Carson
then driven back
after years of starving
And then in the modern
times
John Colley
tried to starve us

Killing off all our animals
I love the Navajos
says Marilyn Monroe Indian
especially this one tall
skinny Navajo
All the Pueblos
love the Navajos
she adds
moving her hips sexy like
and puckering her lips
That's what I love about her
says Skeleton Indian
she's got a wild imagination

His Head

His head
was swatted off
by a grizzly bear
That was new
for his dreams
Normally
his head
was blown off
by some
careless hunter
or vindictive
person
He had seen
the grizzly
coming
but when you see
your destiny
come
barreling
down at you
like that
Two thousand pounds
of mad bear
What can you do
Duck
he thought
too late

In His Dream

In his dream
his head
was blown off
just as he was
sitting down
by the camp fire
to eat
some of the bear
he had killed
that morning
Who shot him
he didn't see
but when he
woke up
he vaguely
remembered
having offended
his wife's brother
Telling him
he wasn't an Indian
but had been
stolen
from the Mormons
out by Sholow
when he was three
years old
That wasn't true
He couldn't
figure out
why in his dreams
he always
came up
with these lies
that kept
getting him
killed

Slow Poke Indian

Slow poke Indian
that's what
he calls himself
If he had been
in the olden times
he says
he would have been
one dead Indian
mighty quick
But these are
modern times
I don't worry much
about being slow
in this
day and time
he says
After all
What's an Indian got
but time
I'm an urban Indian
he says
I don't got
the olden ways
I dress up
and I go out
for a walk
And I smoke
a cigarette
And if I got the money
I buy some beer
I'm a retired
Indian, he says
I've gotten older
than I ever wanted
to be
Even slow poke
as I've been
Even I've gotten
old

Weren't You Ashamed

Weren't you ashamed
in your dream
that you were
the only Indian
shot
by Lt. Emory
in his long march
from Missouri
to San Diego
Was he attacking
General Kearny
asked Lt. Emory
No Sir
said Lt. Emory
Was he posing
a threat
General Kearny
then asked
No Sir
said Lt. Emory
Then why
in God's name
did you shoot
this pitiful
Indian
It was a mistake
Lt. Emory
explained
He saw you sitting
in the distance
and took you
to be a stump
of wood
He thought
If that stump
was an attacking
wild Indian
I'd shoot him
like this

And then your head
was blown off
You were pretty angry
when you woke up
from that dream
Now you're even
getting shot
by mistake
and by a cartographer
to boot

All the Indians

All the Indians
hang out
here
This Albuquerque
night spot
Not as fun
as a powwow
on top of
Sandia mountains
Indian women
from all over
come to dance
That's what
I like
about the powwow
and the mountains
the way they
are
in the night
Great dancing
shapes
of ancestors
And all the time
I'm drinking
to them
and dancing
too
Here
in this
number 1
Albuquerque
night spot

Here Comes Skeleton

Here comes Skeleton
Indian
back to the bar
All his friends
greet him
How come we only
see you at night
someone asks him
Night's my time
he says
Everybody agrees
It's the only time
Women try to get
Skeleton Indian
to dance
and he dances
a bit
Love me honey
the women say
He lets them go
then
I can't love no one
he says
Not a woman
nor a dog
nor a flower
His honesty
drives the women
wild
They embrace
his ribs
caress his
cheek bones
Try to nibble
on the absent
earlobes

You're sure
the hardest man
to make love to
they say
Skeleton Indian
doesn't encourage them
He's just
who he is

He's Had a Drink

He's had a drink
and he's heading home
Skeleton Indian
he knows what
he's doing
Staying away
from the second
that inevitably
leads to more
Skeleton Indian
he stops by every day
has a can of beer
drinks it slow
talks to everyone
All his buddies
are offering
to buy him more
But he shakes his
bony head
His empty eye sockets
are hidden by sunglasses
One thing you can say
about that bony Indian
others chuckle
He knows how to dress
And he does
Stetson with an
eagle feather
silk cowboy shirt
Calvin Klein blue jeans
Handmade boots
from El Paso
When he walks by
the women stop
and stare
He's something
they whisper
He knows his limit
one beer

Never drunk
He looks and feels
good
For a skeleton
that is

Skeleton Indian Doesn't Hate

Skeleton Indian
doesn't hate
anything worse
than not being able
to fall off
to sleep
The dead don't sleep
so peaceful
he says
In fact
most of the time
we can't sleep
at all
It's horrible
he moans
All the world's asleep
and you
you just toss
and turn
and recall everything
you've done
for the last
twenty years
and more
And then you start
thinking of it
all over again
And then you have to
make up things
to think about
I've thought of reading
to pass the time
he says
but then I think
I'm dead
none of this stuff
is interesting
any more
Nothing you living

people do
is interesting
But sleep
that's another matter
Enjoy while you can
is all I can say
because when you're dead
you'll see
The dead don't sleep
so peaceful

There's Nothing Worse

There's nothing worse
than not being able
to fall off to sleep
That's what Skeleton Indian
thinks
He's been dead long enough
to know
that sleep doesn't come
easily to the dead
In fact
it's a mystery to them
how the living
can drop off to sleep
so easily
When you think of the dead
Skeleton Indian says
you probably think
they have it easy
Death's like being asleep
forever except
without dreams
that's what
you probably think
Don't believe it
You've spent one night
being unable to sleep
Try an eternity of it
Skeleton Indian moans

Head Blown Off

Head blown off
4:30
in the afternoon
And you were looking
forward
to something
good to eat
after not eating
since early morning
It's not safe
anymore
for an Indian
you had been
thinking
a minute earlier
And you never know
when someone
in your own tribe
is going
to turn
against you
especially after
the price put
on your head
(preferably not
in one piece)
What is it
that you did
anyway
that got you
on wanted posters
Not everyone can read
but they can see
your picture
and the dollar sign
So what if
it was only
$1 on your head

The dumb ass
who shot you
wouldn't know
until he
tried to collect
Shit, a dollar
he'd say
That's hardly worth
the bullet
Such dreams you have
such crazy
stupid dreams

Dead Indian

Dead Indian
outside
Gallup
after the Indian
rodeo
And a young Indian
too
Blood encrusted
on his clothes
Dead for a day
or two
Was drinking
with his buddies
They're gone
some place
on racing
pickups
down dirt roads
always leading back
to the same
place

Head Blown Off

Head blown off
3rd time
in one dream
Wasn't bad enough
that he was always
getting his head
blown off
each night
Now it's happening
3, 4, 8 times
a night
Dreams sneak up on him
with another episode
of untimely death
And in these dreams
he's got
movie star faces
In one dream
John Wayne's
Humphrey Bogart's
and Rock Hudson's
faces
took turns
getting blown off
his shoulder
And even once
Marilyn Monroe's
face
took its turn
That was the biggest shame
not only because
it was a woman's face
but because he loved
her more
than any other woman
no matter that she
had died
when he was a little boy

When he wakes up
he thinks
Who is this
who's shooting stars
in my dreams
It was bad enough
that they were shooting
me
Now they're shooting
all my
idols

We're Tired of This

We're tired of this
the Indian says
carrying a hatchet
You would think
a hundred mounted
Apaches were behind him
the way he talks
Still, seeing the hatchet
I let him talk
We're tired, I tell you
he says
I agree with him
and say
There's plenty to be
tired about
You don't know what
I'm talking about
he says getting angrier
I agree with him
I don't know what
he's talking about
So what are you tired about
I finally say
The whole mess of it
he says
I'm tired
of the whole mess of it
I see, I say
You don't see, he says
I don't want you seeing
what I see
Why don't you put down
that hatchet, I say
and we'll talk about
what's got you
so angry
He doesn't put down
the hatchet

He's on the warpath
Scalping a Mexican
isn't going to make
anything better, I say
Scalp, he says
as mad as I've ever seen
an Indian get
The French started
the scalping business
I want you out of my land
pronto, he says
and take all them foreigners
with you
I saw my opportunity
and left
but not too far

Skeleton Indian Is in a Deep

Skeleton Indian
is in a deep
and dark mood
Marilyn Monroe
Indian
must have
left him
people whisper
No
it wasn't that
but he wasn't
talking
It's just
that at times
he'd realize
that he was dead
and there was
no remedy
for that

He Is the Runner

He is the runner
with many feet
The runner
without exhaustion
As if he were
three thousand people
The world
has grown old
and dry
since he began running
The only remaining
green plants
are those he holds
in his hand
If we could only get him
to stop
we could convince him
to let us have
the green plants
for our farming
But he will not
stop running
and we cannot catch
him
Where are you running to
we yell at him
Why don't you stop
We will give you
a wife
and a house
We will give you
our friendship
But within minutes
he is beyond
the reach
of our voices
The runners
take after him
but they will never
reach him
Not him
with the many feet

They Were the Four Runners

They were the four runners
Three of them were painted
in red
and the fourth
was the one he clutched
in a hand
Sheaves of young corn plants
The green growing earth
running with them
The three red men
Relatives of the red ants
They were bringing this
to the people
from the long way of winter
They were running
into the spring
and the summer

Night Comes

Night comes
with footsteps
dancing
It has forsaken
its wings
to come dancing
with us
Awaken
to the night
and come dancing
The night
is well proportioned
like an able dancer
See how lightly
the night dances
Night comes
with footsteps
dancing

II

That Time They Sent Us

That time they sent us
to Bosque Redondo
says Skeleton Indian
they said
it was
to make Pueblos
out of us
That's how they called
it
Teach us how to farm
and they'd make
Pueblos
out of us
And the Mescaleros too
Make the land safe
for settlers
I wasn't born then
says Skeleton Indian
but I heard stories
of it
How the people
didn't want to go there
and be made Pueblos
Some Navajos said
We'd rather stay
on our land
even if it means
we'll be dead
But when Kit Carson
came to get us
in Canyon de Chelly
the people
were on the verge
of starving
We'd heard
how they had done in
the Mescaleros

Giving them liquor
and tobacco
then shooting them
Don't you surrender to us
those white soldiers said
We're out
to get you dead
It was the end
of the world
in Canyon de Chelly
and the people
they've never recovered
from that
That and John Collier

That's John Colley

That's John Colley
he said
I looked where
he was pointing
and only caught a flash
of something
dark
What was that
I said
A mouse
or a rat
Neither
he laughed
That was John Colley
I thought about this
looking
at the juniper bushes
where the rodent
had disappeared
You mean
John Collier
I finally said
That's him
the Navajo laughed
You know
I almost didn't talk
to you
he said
When you drove up
I sent one of my kids
to check
your license plate
and he came back
whispering
It's no Colley plate
It's then I thought
he don't work
for the government

He's just a harmless
Mexican
Colley
I kept thinking
driving back home
Sounds like something
a Navajo
would say

You a Mexican

You a Mexican
he said
I looked up
to see
who was talking
Indian
wearing a cowboy hat
cigarette
in his mouth
What's that
growing
out of your head
I said
Is that what
cigarette smoking
does to you
It's a hat
he said
not amused
A hat, I said
sounding surprised
I thought they were
your ears
gone weird
He looked at me
hard like
His eyelids
narrowing
You stupid Mexicans
he said
You don't know
ears from a
hat
I looked at him
square in the face
I don't like Indians
wearing cowboy hats
I said

I don't like
cowboy hats
period
I said
I'm surprised you've lived
as long as you have
he said
Talking as you do
I smiled
and said
Don't be so serious
He kept staring at me
and I kept staring back
You cowboy Indians
I finally said
I don't understand
you
What's to understand
he said
out of the corner
of his mouth
His eyes
now
little slits
sharp as knives
Forget it
I said
and turned
to my beer
But I could feel him
still staring at me
breathing hard
He wanted
some action
I'd of given
it
to him
but I couldn't figure out
who I wanted
to give it to worse
cowboys or Indians

Marilyn Monroe Indian in a Tub

Marilyn Monroe
Indian
in a tub
full
of soap bubbles
She's laughing
at the craziness
of it
Was a time
she says
I'd take my baths
in rain puddles
And some summers
when there wasn't any rain
for weeks
I'd do without
But I was a little girl
and I didn't mind
not bathing
The older people
they'd say
You're smelling
purty good
today
and they'd all laugh
That's why I left
the reservation
and became famous
She smiles
in her tub
full of soap bubbles
and warm water
They don't know
what was underneath
all that dirt
She laughs
lifting out one long
bare leg
as lovely and tantalizing
as any
the world has seen

No Longer Having

No longer having
his head blown off
in his dreams
was a welcome relief
to him
His dreams now
were the typical kind
About reservation life
or Indian school
or living the life
of an urban Indian
Soon he began
to wonder
Am I alive
or am I dreaming it all
And then he began
to suspect
that the only time
he was alive
was when
he was getting
his head blown off
Those weren't dreams
he began to think
That was real life
It was the death
of all the Indians
of America
that he was
living
And now that he didn't
get his head
blown off
any more
he became deeply
saddened
No more Indians
to kill
he thought

It must mean
all the Indians
were dead
and he was having
a death dream
So this is what
it's like
he thought
being dead
and dreaming

Forward and On

Forward and on
the Indian nations
shall rise
out of their graves
all of them looking
like Catlin's drawings
of Indians
It is true
at one time
all Indians
did look alike
The U.S. Army
kept thinking
didn't we just
shoot that Indian
Ammo was cheap
back then
When the red Indian
came charging
at the United States
Army in Missouri
on his purple horse
the soldiers
had to pause
to scratch their heads
before they fired
It was the first time
they had seen
such a thing
No, sir
they kept mumbling
we never shot
this Indian before
And when he fell down
dead
by their feet
they knew
they were making
progress

Everybody regretted
shooting
the purple horse
A purple horse
they said
Now that's
something
special

Now He Doesn't Know

Now he doesn't know
what to do
His head not getting
blown off
and all
He tells his grandchildren
Was a time
I dreamed
great nations
of Indians
except they were all
getting killed off
How were they
getting killed off
his grandchildren
would ask him
Their heads
he'd say
Their heads
kept getting blown up
by gun fire
or attacked
by wild animals
His grandchildren
would get scared
hearing his stories
and they'd start dreaming
the dreams he had
Each time he'd see them
he'd ask
And what were your dreams
last night
Our heads
they'd say
were blown off
And each time
they'd explain
a new way
in which their heads

had blown off
And he just whistled
in amazement
Imagine that
he'd say
I never had my head
blown off
like that
And he felt reassured
As long as there are Indians
dying
he thought
it means
there are Indians
living

It Was the End

It was the end
of the trail
Skeleton Indian
had had
a six-pack and a half
Normally he only
had one beer
He went home
to Marilyn Monroe Indian
cussing everyone
in the bar
as he left
You drunken Indians
he yelled
What you going
to amount to
in this
white man's world
getting drunk
all the time
He staggered on home
End of the trail
he thought
reaching his door
But it was locked
He pounded on the door
but Marilyn
wouldn't open
Finally he put a fist
through a window
and yelled
If I was a live Indian
I'd be bleeding now
I called the cops
Marilyn yelled back
Just then a police car
drove up
with its cherry light
flashing

You're under arrest
the policemen said
Aren't you Navajos
Skeleton Indian asked
steadying himself
against the house
We are
they said
Are you going to shoot me
if I don't surrender
Skeleton laughed
a drunken laugh
If we have to
they said nervously
Skeleton Indian
staggered
in their direction
The cops started firing
but the bullets went
through empty air
They got in their car
and took off quick
Then Marilyn opened the door
You still drunk
she said
No
They sobered me up
Skeleton Indian said
contritely
Then you can
come in
Marilyn said
What's the matter with you
You promised
you'd only drink
one beer
I know, he said
but I got to let loose
once in a while
Marilyn hugged him tight
You crazy Indian
she said

As long
as you don't beat me
I'll love you
through eternity

Love and Death

Love and death
they're similar
Skeleton Indian
knows about them
Marilyn Monroe Indian
I love her
he says
but she's dead
and so am I
What about lovemaking
I ask
You serious, he says
looking at me
with a bigger smile
than usual
I've seen you two kiss
so I wondered
I say
Kiss, he says
laughing
We sure got you fooled
Lips
You need lips
to kiss
Do we look
like we have lips
Two old skeletons
like us
That's true, I say
You don't have lips
But I swear
I've seen you kiss
Skeleton Indian
laughs again
Marilyn, he yells
Marilyn, come talk
to this fool
I see her coming
from the other room

but I stand up
and leave
Embarrassed
enough
as it is

Blessed Is the Blue Man

Blessed is the blue man
he says
Blue man
with government hat
he says
Are you surrendering
says the blue man with
the hat
I is
says the old Indian
And your tribe
says the blue man
What are their intentions
Their intentions
says the Indian
are to surrender
if you will accept surrender
Well, let me see
says the blue man
How does it benefit me
to accept
your surrendering
Seems expensive to me
Not expensive
says the old Indian
We just need water
and a few ounces
of food
each month
not expensive
Seems to me it is
says the blue man
My horses need water
and my men
like to eat
So you don't accept
our surrendering
says the Indian
Go back to your people

says the blue man
and tell them this
I say
if you live or die
You come
or I come after you
It's all the same to me
But our women and children
What will become of them
says the old Indian
The Utes can have them
says the blue man
The Indian
walks away slowly
Tell them this
the blue man yells
after him
They've got four hours
to decide

Be Appeased

Be appeased
Take from this hand
an offering
My heart
It is all
I have to offer
Take it
and I will stop
breathing
You have covered
the land
in a blue
ominous shadow
I have heeded it
Be appeased
Take this offering
My heart
my breathing

He Was Approached

He was approached
by the great
blue shadow
of a man
I'm from Washington
he said
How's Lincoln
the Indian asked
Dead
the blue shadow
said
Sorry to hear that
said the Indian
How long has
he been dead
Over a hundred years
said the blue shadow
growing larger
and more ominous
as it approached
The Indian got
down
on his knees
We only have
a few acres left
are you going
to take that
he said
We done took it
a long time ago
the blue shadow said
I'm here to see
you stay off
Where am I to go
said the Indian
But the blue shadow
had grown too big
to be talked to

As far as the Indian
could see
the land
had turned blue
Not only the dirt
but the grass
and the trees
This is what's come
of Lincoln's dying
the Indian moaned
Looking around
seeing every way
was the same
blue way
of going
and not returning

Oh, No

Oh, no
It's starting
all over
A respite of
two weeks
Dreamless sleep
or anyway
he didn't
remember anything
And here it goes
The purple
welling up
from the earth
surrounding him
And then
his teeth
go flying
His head
is one great
cavity
Darkness visited me
he thinks
too late
Fragments of his
skull
disappearing
in a yellow sky
And not even
a shot fired
this time
His head blown up
in long delayed
anticipation

Marilyn Monroe Indian
She's an Angel

Marilyn Monroe Indian
She's an angel
See those lips
Angel lips
Always her mouth
slightly open
Her lips moist
Even in this
dry country
Marilyn Monroe Indian
is as pale white
as dry desert clouds
That's what you imagine
when you first see her
But she's a skeleton
Can't you see
Like Skeleton Indian
She's been dead
twenty years
and more
Her lips are a mirage
you can say
Men dying for love
spot them right away
They want to drink
of her lips
Be made whole again
In their eyes
She is the perfect
beauty
And Marilyn
At first she is
gladdened
by their wanting her
But then
her mood changes
she grows depressed

All she can do
is flirt with them
Nothing more
is possible
They are alive
and she is dead
She would kill herself
at the impossible
situation of it all
if she wasn't
already dead

III

Who Was He

Who was he
says Skeleton Indian
He was nobody
says Marilyn Monroe
Indian
No, who was he
repeats
Skeleton Indian
He was a poet
Marilyn says
as if she were
disgusted
A poet
Skeleton Indian
laughs
Can you imagine
Marilyn Monroe
Indian laughs
too
No wonder he died
and young too
Skeleton Indian says
He was sad
wasn't he
Marilyn says
growing pensive
Yes, he was
Skeleton Indian
suddenly says
Marilyn Monroe Indian
says
I suppose so
Expressionless
And him, she says
I could have loved him
Of course
if I didn't already
love you

I understand
Skeleton Indian
says
I could have loved
him too
The sadness of him
The poetry that was
so much of him
that it killed him
I suspected as much
Marilyn says
You really think it was
the poetry
that done
him in
He was a beautiful
child
she says
without thinking
A child
Skeleton Indian
nods in agreement
We'll miss him
he adds

Welcome, Says Skeleton

Welcome, says Skeleton
Indian to Ray
Welcome
Raymond
says Marilyn Monroe Indian
How you liking death
asks Skeleton Indian
as if I didn't know
I been expecting it
Ray says
I'm at a loss
for words
And you a poet
Marilyn says astonished
When I heard
you were coming
to this reservation
I was glad
I thought
He'll put it in words
what we're experiencing
and I'll make
my peace
with death
but I should
have known it
words fail us
once we are dead
I told you
Skeleton Indian says
Poets don't know
anything more
about death
than any other
dead person

So, What's Death Like Ray

So, what's death like Ray
says Skeleton Indian
It's like perfect silence
Raymond says without hesitation
It *is* deathly quiet
Skeleton Indian says
I've known as much
What *else* can you tell me Ray
It's like love, Raymond says
How's that, says Skeleton
It's like love that was good
and is now over, says Raymond
I *see*, says Skeleton Indian
I can *see* you've been a lover
in your brief life
Brief and too long, says Raymond
Too many calls for help
and when I called it was
Can't talk now, will call you back
So, this is all there is to death
says Skeleton Indian
That and humiliation, says Raymond
and forever being some other place

Well Look

Well look
who's here
still with us
Uncle Owl
says Skeleton Indian
Is that his name
Or is it Uncle
Washington D. C.
Neither, says
Marilyn Monroe
Indian
Can't you see
it's just Raymond
It's Uncle
Death
says Skeleton
Indian
See how he
just
sits there
staring at us
You're wearing out
your welcome
says Skeleton
Where's he to go
says Marilyn
He's lost
can't you see
Let his people
take him in
says Skeleton Indian
You hear him
says Marilyn
Monroe Indian
Get on
to your people
You're cute enough
but all you do
is stare

You heard her
says Skeleton Indian
get on out of here
You outwore
your welcome
Where, where
are my people
stutters
Raymond
I'm afraid if I leave
I won't find them
and then I'll be
eternally
alone
Skeleton Indian
laughs
You *don't* think
you're alone with us
Brother
you've got something
to learn
about being
dead

Raymond, Raymond

Raymond, Raymond
Raymond
says Skeleton Indian
Won't you stop
staring at me
Yes, you are dead
Can't you see
He's in shock
Marilyn Monroe
Indian
says
Is that what
it is
says Skeleton Indian
How'd he land up
with us
says Marilyn Monroe Indian
I thought this reservation
was only for Indians
A mistake
I suppose
says Skeleton Indian

Raymond

Raymond
Raymond, Raymond
Raymond
Raymond, Raymond
says Marilyn Monroe
Indian
I love
the frown
on your forehead
I love your chin
I love
your eyebrows
I love your
plaid shirt
Hold on
says Skeleton Indian
What's this
happening
between you
and Ray
If it's love
I'll
I'll
You'll what
says Marilyn
You'll
kill him
You stupid Navajo
she says
He's a dead man
just like
you are
Don't call me
a stupid Navajo
you stupid
Pueblo
says Skeleton Indian

Raymond
sneaks away
and listens
from a distance
It's like
being alive
he thinks
remembering
when he was a child
and waking up
to hear
his parents arguing
As an adult
waking up
to hear friends
in the kitchen
talking on the edge
of things
Waking up as an adult
to situations
he thought
were nightmares
Where's Raymond
says Marilyn
You chased him
away
Skeleton Indian
smirks
He don't love you
he adds
Marilyn Monroe Indian
grows desperate
I'm just beginning
to realize
how dead
I really am
she says

Raymond, Say You Love Me

Raymond, say you love me
says Marilyn Monroe Indian
Skeleton Indian won't mind
as long as it's just talk
I've been hurt too much by love
to make fun of it, says Raymond
It doesn't hurt to amuse
ourselves a little bit, says Marilyn
Ever since you came here
we haven't seen anyone but you
Why is that, she says turning
to Skeleton Indian
He's ruined things for us
says Skeleton Indian
Before he came we found ways
of mingling with the living
They loved us and we, well
we appreciated them
It was something to do
And Ray ruined it
I don't know how he did it
but he did
How did you do it, Raymond
asks Marilyn Monroe Indian
How did you alienate us
from the living
What powers
of death do you have
and why
did you bring them to us
And why don't you take
them away with you
says Skeleton
It's not my doing
says Raymond
I didn't wish to come here
Maybe you brought me here
he says

I should be the one to be upset
Marilyn Monroe Indian and Skeleton
Indian grow deathly quiet
They realize what he said is true
They don't fully understand
the truth of it
But enough

Raymond Is in Love

Raymond is in love
with Marilyn Monroe
Indian
I love you
he finally says
when Skeleton Indian
is out of hearing
I even love your shoes
says Raymond
I love you so much
I love the fake
glass diamonds
on the tips
of your shoes
Marilyn is pleased
I love you too
she says
I even love
Well, I love you all
But don't say anything
to Skeleton Indian
That'd depress him worse
than he already is
Ever since you came
everything's changed
for the worse for him
and for me too
until I heard you say
you loved me
that is
I do, Marilyn
I do love you
Honestly
says Raymond
Let's hope he doesn't
come back
for a while
says Marilyn Monroe
Indian

Keep looking at me
that way
Keep looking at me
as if you really
love me
But if you ever say
anything
to Skeleton Indian
I swear
I'll deny it all

Skeleton Indian and Marilyn

Skeleton Indian
and Marilyn Monroe Indian
are leaving
where they were
to seek out the world
of the living
Which way is out
says Marilyn
It all looks the same
way of going
to me
Whichever way
says Skeleton Indian
We have to do something
I think we're going
to lose the world
for good
if we don't do something
We should have brought
Ray
says Marilyn Monroe Indian
You saw how sad he looked
like a dog
you had just kicked
He was born
with that look
on his face
says Skeleton Indian
We shouldn't have left
him
alone, says Marilyn
He'll never find
anyone
He'll wander alone
No one to talk to
No one to see
You love him, don't you
says Skeleton Indian
Marilyn grows quiet

You see why
we had to leave him
says Skeleton Indian
You would have loved him
so much
in time
that one day
you both
would have left me
alone
We never would have
done that
says Marilyn Monroe
Indian
The love I have for you
if forever
it's the only alive
thing
we have between us
You were hard
on Raymond
Marilyn suddenly says
Go back to him
if that's how you feel
says Skeleton Indian
I'll find the world
on my own
I don't know where
we've come to already
says Marilyn
I don't know
where we were
We've come too far
Raymond, Raymond
Where are you Raymond
Marilyn Monroe Indian
looks about
at nothingness
Sees and hears nothing
He is lost
says Marilyn
And we are lost too

she adds
Come on this way
says Skeleton Indian
We haven't been this way
It all looks the same
way of going
to me
says Marilyn Monroe
Indian

It's All the Same Way

It's all the same way
of going
and not arriving
says Marilyn Monroe Indian
I think we've been walking
a million years
says Skeleton Indian
A million since
we last saw Raymond
says Marilyn
You don't forget
says Skeleton
I love you deeply
says Marilyn
I wouldn't have been
wandering with you
for a million years
if I didn't
But I had come to love
Raymond, too
When you're dead
you realize how precious
love can be
Why didn't you let me love
both of you, Marilyn sighs
Maybe I should have
says Skeleton Indian
You really mean that
says Marilyn Monroe Indian
It couldn't be any worse
than wandering about
for a million years
says Skeleton Indian
We'll find Raymond
says Marilyn
newly invigorated
Even if it takes
another million years

Raymond, Says Marilyn Monroe

Raymond
says Marilyn Monroe
Indian
Where've you been
We've been looking for you
for a million and a half
years
And now we find you
Where *you* been
says Raymond
I turned my back
on you two
one day
a long time ago
and then you're gone
I haven't moved
I've been here
all the time
says Raymond
Marilyn takes Raymond
off a ways
where Skeleton
can't hear them
He says I can love you
say Marilyn
You'll love me
says Raymond
astonished
If you did
death wouldn't be so bad
I've loved you deeply
all this time
says Marilyn Monroe Indian
Let's leave
just you and I
says Raymond
Many years I wanted
to leave
and explore

but I thought
you'd come back
so I just waited
Let's leave
But it's all the same
out there
says Marilyn
There's no place
that's different
Death's all the same
At least
we'll be away
from Skeleton Indian
says Raymond
He won't find us
The happiness
that had filled
Marilyn Monroe Indian's
face
is gone
He said I'd leave him
says Marilyn
if I truly came
to love you

He Comes Wide

He comes wide
in a wave of
blue
and white
His hair is blue
and there is blood
on his lips
His body is a flag
unfurling
Unfurling great
as the land
He comes
and you recognize
him
as mountains
and as the tiny
blue sheep
on the mountains
And you recognize
him
as wanting
But he is dying
Even as great
and splendid
as he is
He is unfurling
himself
and dying

Night Comes with Footsteps

Night comes
with footsteps
dancing
It has descended on us
and has forsaken
its wings
to come dancing
with us
Awaken
Hear us
Awaken
to the night
Come dancing
Night has many
legs and feet
The night
is well proportioned
like an able dancer
See how lightly
the night raises
its feet
Night comes
with footsteps
dancing
It has long
watched us
out of the shadows
Now it comes dancing
Hear us
We are so quiet
you would think
we were feathers
in the air
Listen
It is in you
This dancing

Born in 1950 in Chacon, New Mexico, Leo Romero grew up in Las Vegas, New Mexico. He has a B.A. in English from the University of New Mexico and an M.A. in English from New Mexico State University. Mr. Romero has received a National Endowment for the Arts fellowship and is a Pushcart Prize winner. He has published two other books of poetry, **Agua Negra** (Ahsahta Press) and **Celso** (University of Houston Press). In 1985, poems from these two books were adapted into a play called "I Am Celso" by The Group, a theatrical company of Seattle, Washington, which has presented it in several states, including New York (for Joseph Papp's Latino Theatre Festival). Mr. Romero has also published two chapbooks, **During the Growing Season** and **Desert Nights.** His poetry has most recently appeared in **New Worlds of Literature** (W.W. Norton, 1989) and **Sotto il Quinto Sole** (Passigli, 1990), an anthology of Chicano poetry published in Italy, and will appear in **After Aztlan: Latino Poets in the Nineties** (David Godine, 1991). His work has been discussed in two texts of criticism, **Understanding Chicano Literature** (University of South Carolina Press, 1988) and **Pasó por Aquí**, critical essays on the New Mexican literary tradition (University of New Mexico Press, 1989). Leo Romero has worked for the Social Security Administration as well as the Los Alamos National Laboratory, where he was a technical writer and in Educational Outreach, presenting science programs in the elementary schools of northern New Mexico. Currently, with the help of his wife, Elizabeth, an artist, he owns and operates a bookstore specializing in fine used books. The store, Books and More Books, is in Santa Fe, New Mexico, as is his home.

Ahsahta Press

MODERN & CONTEMPORARY POETRY
OF THE AMERICAN WEST

Donald Schenker, *Up Here*
Richard Speakes, *Hannah's Travel*
Genevieve Taggard, *To the Natural World*
*Marnie Walsh, *A Taste of the Knife*
Bill Witherup, *Men at Work*
*Carolyne Wright, *Stealing the Children*

Women Poets of the West: An Anthology, 1850-1950

*Selections from these volumes, read by their authors, are available on *The Ahsahta Cassette Sampler*.